LISTEN HEAR

Book 1

Ear Training & Warmups for Singers, Songwriters and Music Lovers!

By Sarah Bonsignore

Published by Sarah Bonsignore BMI
Founder, Directory of SingPlayStudios LLC, Brentwood, TN
Printed on acid-free paper

SingPlayStudios.com sarahbonsignore.org
Fearless Rose Publishing BMI

For my teachers and students, thank you
for inspiring me to do what I love ♫♪

Dear Music Lovers,

2020 was a scary and confusing year for most of us, and early on (after weeks of worry, confusion and binge-watching bad TV) I decided I needed a reason to get out of my pajamas and do something productive, so I began making lesson videos for my children and students. The learning curve was steep and exhausting, but over the next year I was able to use logic and video editing software more proficiently, and it excited me that my children and students seemed to be enjoying the tutorials. By 2022 I realized I had a whole lot of content and so I decided to create a book form for some of the exercises and warmups. Hence, "Listen Hear" Book 1 for beginners.

Unit 1 is a compilation of ear training exercises that are designed to teach the intervals from a 2nd to an octave. Each lesson video has backing tracks at the end so that you can practice at your leisure. I plan to have the mp3s available on my website singplaystudios.com by the end of 2022 so that students can download the exercises to their devices and practice on the go. That's the plan anyway!

Unit 2 is a collection of simple warmups for beginners. Use the warmups to enhance your sight-reading skills and to gently develop vocal range and confidence. Find a comfortable range to practice in, and if you feel like your voice is being strained, stop singing! If you have any questions and concerns, reach out to me on instagram @singplaystudios or at singplaystudios.com. Sign up is free!

Music is my happy place, and my hope is that this book gets you listening more deeply, singing more confidently, and composing the music that is already inside you. Stay open to the process and have patience, and don't forget to practice a few times a week. Music is in our DNA, and you can do this!

Yours,

Sarah Bonsignore
Founder, Director
SingPlayStudios

Contents

Unit A: Beginner Ear Training

Unit B: Vocal Warm-Ups

A brief introduction

A slightly longer introduction! My husband thought this one was too long at 4 minutes, but for those of you who are interested in how the book idea was born in 2020, feel free to watch!

UNIT A

Echo Me

Ear Training Wamup

Sarah Bonsignore
SingPlayStudios.com

*Once you are familiar with the exercise, try singing it again leaving out the numbers 2 and 4 (re and fa)

* Now try singing the exercise leaving out all the quarter notes!

Interval Practice
Seconds

Sarah Bonsignore
SingPlayStudios Nashville

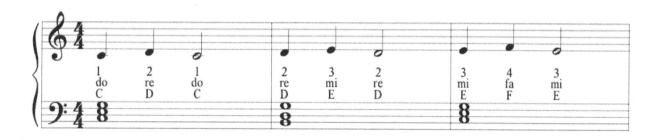

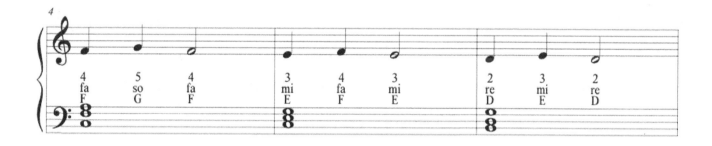

TAKE 🎵 In music, 1 is the same as 8 (the notes are just an octave apart) hence singing 1-7-1 at the end.

Interval Practice Thirds

Sarah Bonsignore
SingPlayStudios

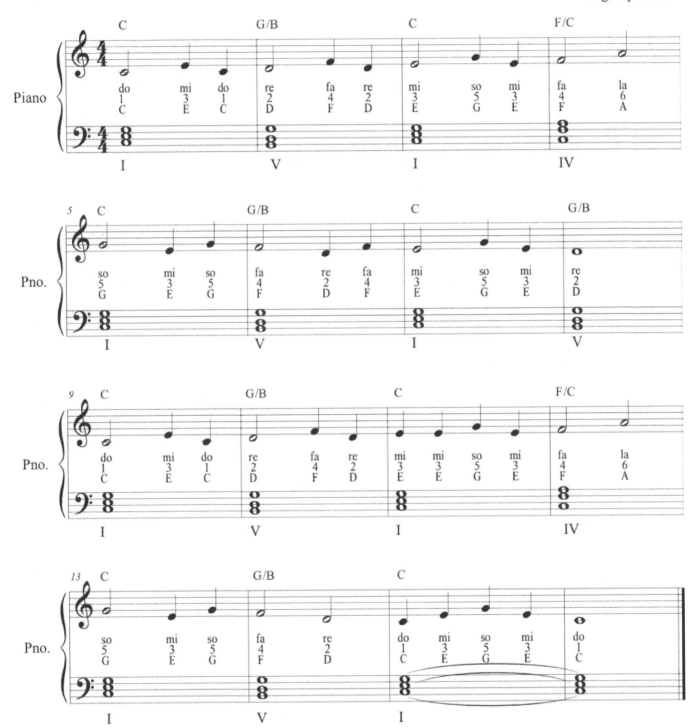

Sight Reading 2nds
Moving by Step

Sarah Bonsignore
SingPlayStudios.com

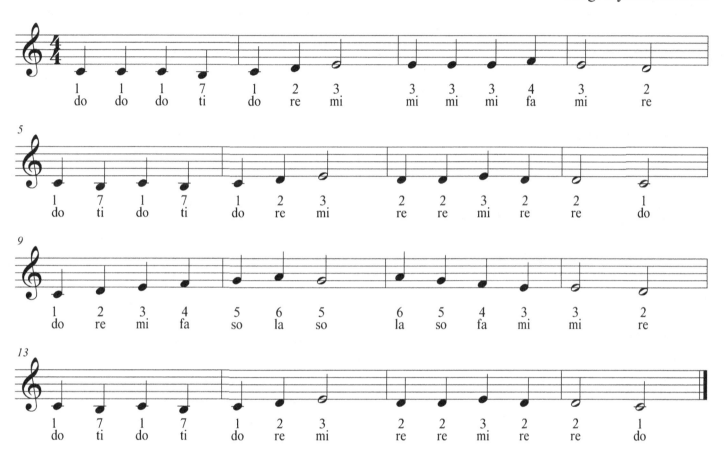

Moving by step ~
Seconds can be "whole steps" or "half steps".
A half step is a minor 2nd and a whole step is
a major 2nd. "Fur Elise" by Beethoven begins
with a half step. The chorus of "Lean On Me" begins
with (descending) whole steps. Hum both melodies to
yourself and start to feel the difference in your voice.

Sight Reading 2nds

Sarah Bonsignore
SingPlayStudios

*READING WITHOUT ALL THE GUIDE NOTES

Sight reading 2nds and 3rds

Sarah Bonsignore
SingPlayStudios.com

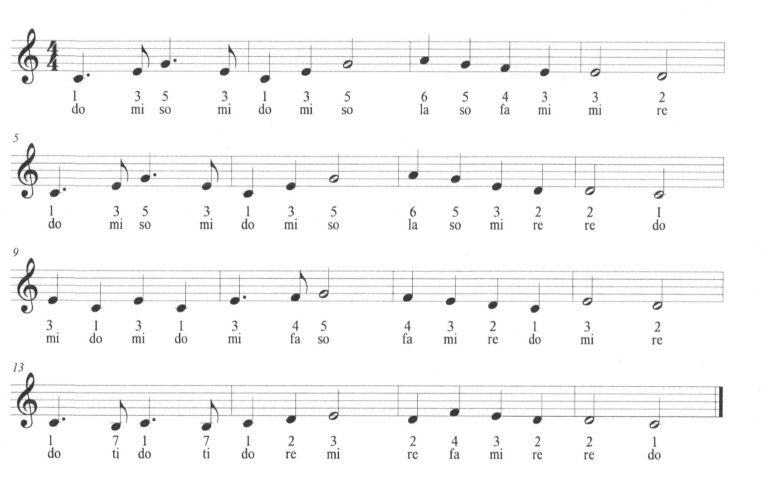

Sight reading 2nds and 3rds

Without Guide Notes

Sarah Bonsignore
SingPlayStudios

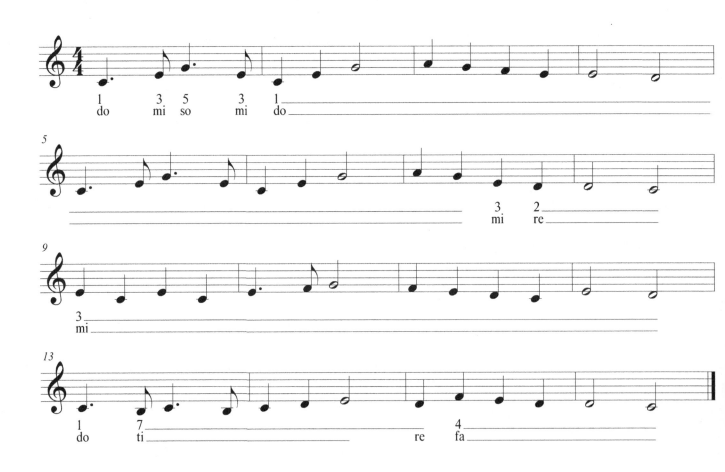

Interval Practice
Fourths

Sarah Bonsignore
SingPlayStudios

Interval Practice
Fifths

Sarah Bonsignore
SingPlayStudios

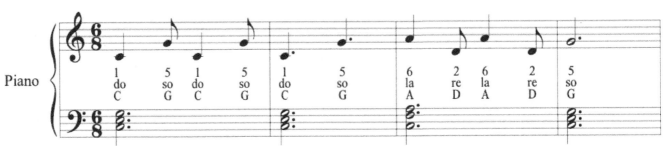

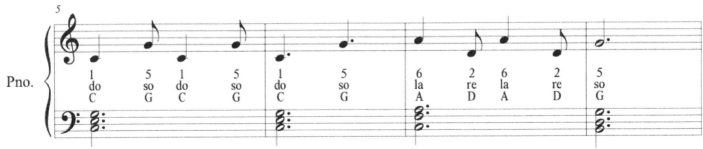

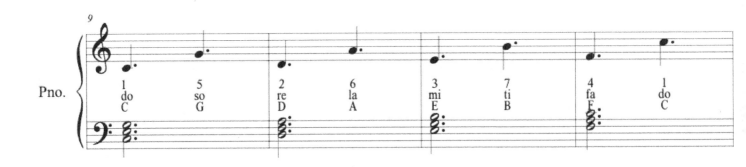

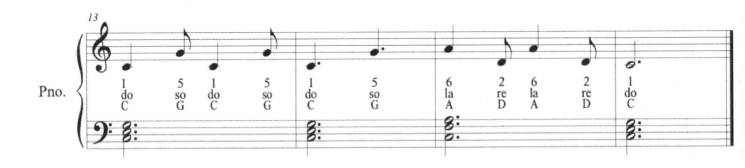

Interval Practice
Sixths

Sarah Bonsignore
SingPlayStudios

18

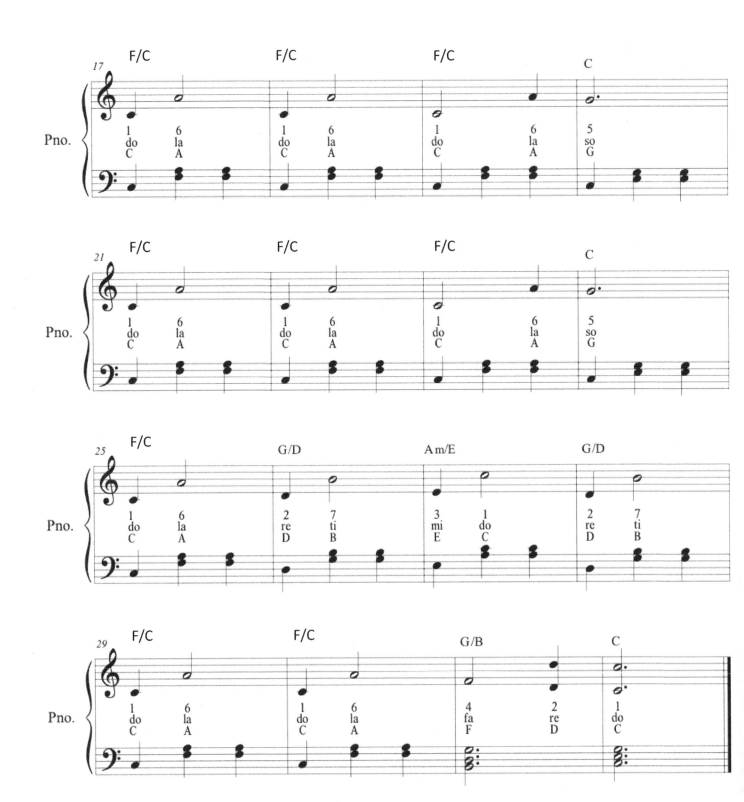

Interval Practice
Sevenths

Sarah Bonsignore
SingPlayStudios

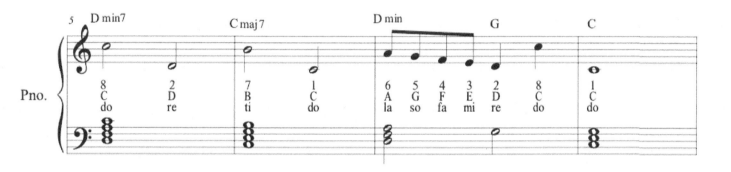

Interval Warmup

Sarah Bonsignore
SingPlayStudios

Interval Warmup
2nds to 8ves

Sarah Bonsignore
SingPlayStudios

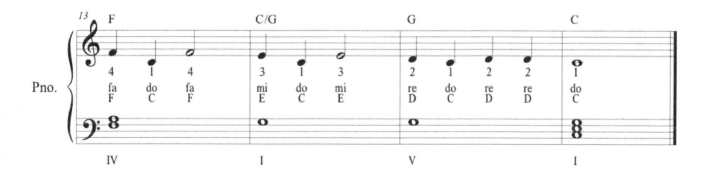

Interval Warmup 1

Sarah Bonsignore
SingPlayStudios

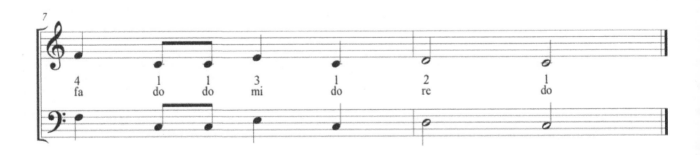

Interval Warmup 1

in G Major

Sarah Bonsignore
SingPlayStudios.com

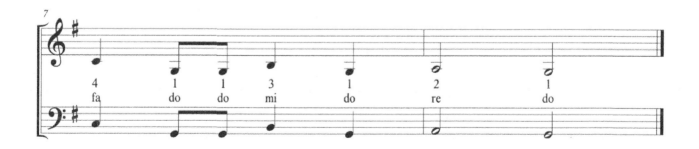

Interval Warmup 1

in A Major

Sarah Bonsignore
SingPlayStudios.com

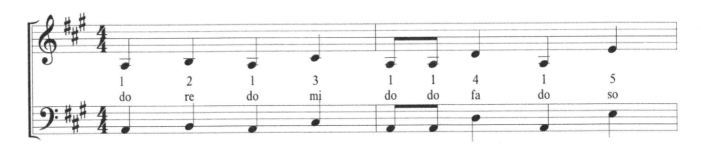

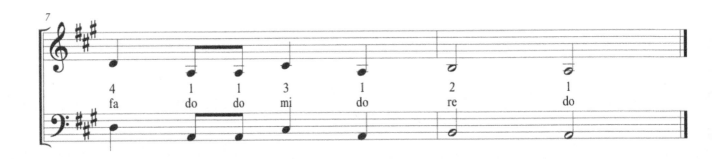

Interval Practice
Octaves (8ve)

Sarah Bonsignore
SingPlayStudios

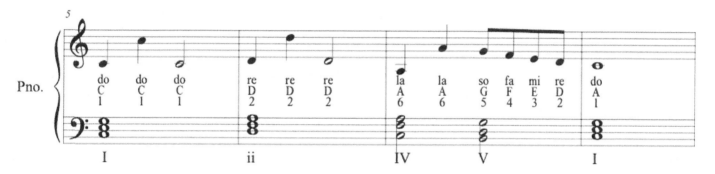

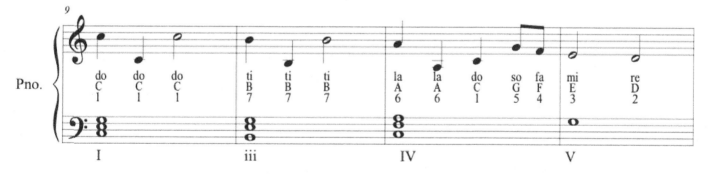

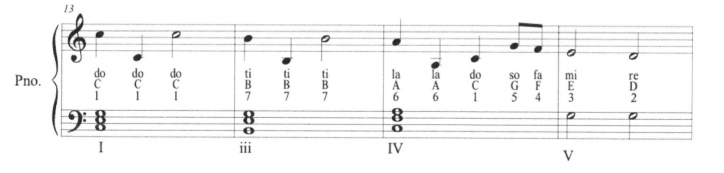

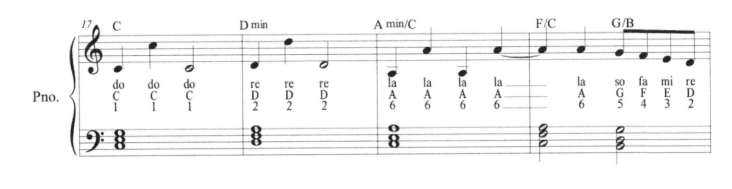

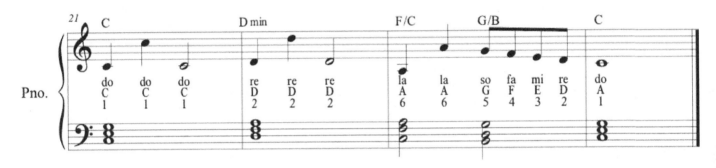

Scales and Arpeggio Warmup

(With Guide Notes)

Sarah Bonsignore
SingPlayStudios

Scales and Arpeggio Warmup

(No Guide Notes)

Sarah Bonsignore
SingPlayStudios

Scale and Arpeggio warmup
in A major

Sarah Bonsignore
SingPlayStudios Nashville

Scale and Arpeggio Warmup in Bb Major

Sarah Bonsignore
SingPlayStudios

UNIT B

Vocal Warmup 1

Moving By Step

Sarah Bonsignore

Ways to try this exercise

1- humming
2 - sing on "ee"
3 - sing on "oo"
4 - lip trill

Vocal Warmup 2
Singing in Thirds

Sarah Bonsignore
SingPlayStudios Nashville

do mi so mi do

Vocal Warmup 3
The Turn and the Trill

Sarah Bonsignore
SingPlayStudios.com

Vocal Warmup 4
The Five Note Scale

Sarah Bonsignore
SingPlayStudios Nashville

Vocal Warmup 5
The Major Arpeggio

Sarah Bonsignore
SingPlayStudios

Vocal Warmup 6

Scale and Arpeggio

Sarah Bonsignore
SingPlayStudios Nashville

Vocal Warmup 7
Breath Control

Sarah Bonsignore
SingPlayStudios Nashville

Voice

Vocal Warmup 8

Running (flexibilty)

Sarah Bonsignore
SingPlayStudios.com

Vocal Warmup 9

Skipping

Sarah Bonsignore
SingPlayStudios Nashville

Vocal Warmup 10

Singing Octaves

Sarah Bonsignore
SingPlayStudios Nashville

Sarah Bonsignore is a South African born American sync artist, composer, educator, and producer. She received her bachelor's degree from the University of Natal, Durban (UKZN), majoring in piano performance, and her master's degree from Mannes College of Music in Manhattan, majoring in voice. Sarah is an award-winning musician who was most recently a finalist in the John Lennon Songwriting Contest. She has also performed both as a soprano soloist and a conductor at Carnegie Hall, and another highlight of her career was performing for Nelson Mandela at his inauguration ball in her hometown of Durban. To date, she has released four albums of original music and many singles which can be heard on all streaming platforms.

After graduating college, Sarah was on the music faculty of the Hackley School in Westchester, NY for eight years. She then joined the faculty of the Trinity School on the Upper West Side of Manhattan for 11 years. During her tenure Sarah taught choirs, directed musical theater, taught AP theory, songwriting, and classroom music. She ran international choral trips, advised students, directed chapel music, and sat on many educational committees. In 2018, Sarah relocated to Nashville with her family to write and produce full time. When the pandemic began, she reinvented herself as an online ear training and piano teacher, vocal coach and a publisher of piano repertoire books. She also founded her own school, SingPlayStudios LLC virtually during the summer of 2020 and began teaching in person during the fall of 2021. Sarah runs local "First Gig" and "SongStarters" programs at her school and for the county and loves teaching adults her "Chords and Cocktails" classes and programming mini songwriting retreats, as well as Nashville shows for aspiring songwriters and musicians.

Sarah is currently on the composer roster for a daytime show, and many of her songs and instrumentals have been heard on TV and radio throughout the US, Canada and South Africa. When she is not making music, she can be found playing tremendously mediocre golf with her talented husband and children and canoeing the beautiful rivers of Tennessee. Sarah believes music and the arts make the world a better place and hopes to bring quality and affordable education and resources to children and adults the whole world over.

Scan here to find Sarah's courses in ear training, beginner piano and voice, and free lesson links and workshops. Sign up is free!

©2022 Sarah Bonsignore BMI

Made in the USA
Coppell, TX
01 March 2023